Vegetarian Recipes in 30 Mi
Family-Friendly Soup, Sala
Breakfast and Dessert Recipes
Inspired by The Mediterranean Diet

by **Vesela Tabakova**
Text copyright(c)2015 Vesela Tabakova

Table Of Contents

Top 70 No-Stress, No-Mess Vegetarian Dinners – Quick Recipes You Can Make On The GO!

Our fast-paced lives leave us with less and less time for food planning and cooking healthy meals. When time is at a premium and all you want is to be with your family, these simple and easy to prepare vegetarian meals will allow you to shorten the amount of time you spend in the kitchen and have a quick weeknight supper or a delicious weekend dinner in an instant.

As a working mother of teenagers who absolutely loves cooking but doesn't have the luxury of long periods in the kitchen, I am constantly looking for new, healthy and fast meatless recipes to add to my everyday menus. Here's a collection of some of my favourite ridiculously quick vegetarian dinners that take less than half an hour to make and won't be a challenge even by the inexperienced cook.

With only about 30 minutes and a couple of your favorite vegetables, legumes, dairy products and aromatic herbs and spices, you can put together a healthy whole food vegetarian meal that will please everyone at the table. If you want to get dinner on the table fast and good nutrition is a must – this cookbook is for you!

Salads and Appetizers

Summer Macaroni Salad

Serves 5-6

Prep time 25 min

Ingredients:

2 cups macaroni pasta

2 hard boiled eggs, chopped

2 roasted red bell peppers, thinly sliced

3-4 spring onions, finely cut

3 tbsp fresh dill, chopped

1/3 cup mayonnaise

2 tbsp lemon juice

freshly ground black pepper, to taste

Directions:

Cook macaroni as directed on package. When cooked through but still slightly firm remove from heat, drain and rinse with cool water.

Put chopped onions into a salad bowl and toss with the lemon juice. Add in macaroni and all the other ingredients. Season with salt and pepper to taste and serve.

Greek Salad

Serves 6

Prep time 5-6 min

Ingredients:

2 cucumbers, diced

2 tomatoes, sliced

1 green lettuce, cut in thin strips

2 red bell peppers, cut

1/2 cup black olives, pitted

3.5 oz feta cheese, cut

1 red onion, sliced

2 tbsp olive oil

2 tbsp lemon juice

salt and ground black pepper, to taste

Directions:

Dice the cucumbers and slice the tomatoes. Tear the lettuce or cut it in thin strips. De-seed and cut the peppers in strips.

Mix all vegetables in a salad bowl. Add the olives and the feta cheese cut in cubes.

In a small cup mix the olive oil and the lemon juice with salt and pepper. Pour over the salad and toss to coat.

Caprese Salad

Serves 6

Prep time 4 min

Ingredients:

4 tomatoes, sliced

6 oz mozzarella cheese, sliced

10 fresh basil leaves

3 tbsp olive oil

2 tbsp red wine vinegar

salt, to taste

Directions:

Slice the tomatoes and mozzarella, then layer the tomato slices, whole fresh basil leaves and mozzarella slices on a plate.

Drizzle olive oil and vinegar over the salad and serve.

Quick Coleslaw

Serves 4

Prep time 5 min

Ingredients:

1/2 Chinese cabbage, shredded

1 green bell pepper, sliced into thin strips

1 carrot, cut into thin strips

4 spring onions, chopped

for the dressing

3 tbsp lemon juice

3 tbsp soy sauce

3 tbsp sweet chilli sauce

Directions:

Remove any damaged outer leaves and rinse the cabbage. Holding cabbage from the base and, starting at the opposite end, shred leaves thinly.

In a salad bowl, combine vegetables. Whisk dressing ingredients and pour over salad. Toss to combine and serve.

Fatoush

Serves 6

Prep time 6-7 min

Ingredients:

2 cups lettuce, washed, dried, and chopped

3 tomatoes, chopped

1 cucumber, peeled and chopped

1 green pepper, deseeded and chopped

1 cup radishes, sliced in half

1 small red onion, finely chopped

half a bunch of parsley, finely cut

2 tbsp finely chopped fresh mint

3 tbsp olive oil

4 tbsp lemon juice

salt and black pepper to taste

2 whole-wheat pita breads

Directions:

Toast the pita breads in a skillet until they are browned and crisp. Set aside. Place the lettuce, tomatoes, cucumbers, green pepper, radishes, onion, parsley and mint in a salad bowl.

Break up the toasted pita into bite-size pieces and add to the salad.

Prepare the dressing by whisking together olive oil with lemon juice, a pinch of salt and some black pepper. Toss to coat and serve.

Chickpea Salad

Serves 4

Prep time 5 min

Ingredients:

1 cup canned chickpeas, drained and rinsed

2 spring onions, thinly sliced

1 small cucumber, diced

2 green bell peppers, chopped

2 tomatoes, diced

2 tbsp chopped fresh parsley

1 tsp capers, drained and rinsed

juice of half lemon

2 tbsp sunflower oil

1 tbsp red wine vinegar

a pinch of dried oregano

salt and pepper, to taste

Directions:

In a medium bowl, toss together chickpeas, spring onions, cucumber, bell pepper, tomato, parsley, and capers.

In a smaller bowl, stir together the remaining ingredients and pour over the chickpea salad. Toss to coat and serve.

Mediterranean Avocado Salad

Serves 5

Prep time 5-6 min

Ingredients

1 avocado, peeled, halved and cut into cubes

1 cup grape tomatoes

1 cup radishes, sliced

2 tbsp drained capers, rinsed

1 large cucumber, quartered and sliced

a handful of rocket leaves

½ cup green olives, pitted, halved

½ cup black olives, pitted, sliced

7-8 fresh basil leaves, torn

2 tbsp olive oil

2 tbsp red wine vinegar

salt and pepper, to taste

Directions:

Place avocado, cucumber, tomatoes, radishes, rocket, olives, capers and basil in a large salad bowl.

Toss to combine then sprinkle with vinegar and olive oil. Season with salt and pepper, toss again and serve.

Avocado and Cucumber Salad

Serves 5

Prep time 5 min

Ingredients

2 avocados, peeled, halved and sliced

2-3 green onions, finely cut

1 cucumber, halved, sliced

1/2 cup cooked sweet corn

for the dressing:

2 tbsp olive oil

3 tbsp lemon juice

1 tbsp Dijon mustard

1/2 cup finely cut dill leaves

salt and pepper, to taste

Directions:

Combine avocado, cucumber, corn and green onions in a deep salad bowl.

Whisk olive oil, lemon juice, dill and mustard until smooth, then drizzle over the salad.

Season with salt and pepper to taste, toss to combine, and serve.

Warm Vitamin Salad

Serves 4

Prep time 15 min

Ingredients

7 oz cauliflower, cut into florets

7 oz baby Brussels sprouts, trimmed

7 oz broccoli, cut into florets

for the dressing:

2 tbsp lemon juice

4 tbsp olive oil

1/2 tsp ginger powder

1/2 cup parsley leaves, very finely cut

Directions:

Cook cauliflower, broccoli and Brussels sprouts in a steamer basket over boiling water for 10 minutes or until just tender. Refresh under cold water for a minute and set aside in a deep salad bowl.

Whisk lemon juice, olive oil and ginger powder in a small bowl. Add in salt and pepper to taste; pour over the salad. Top with parsley and serve.

Apple, Walnut and Radicchio Salad

Serves 4-5

Prep time 6-7 min

Ingredients

1 radicchio, trimmed, finely shredded

2 apples, quartered and thinly sliced

a handful of rocket leaves

4-5 green onions, chopped

1/2 cup walnuts, halved and toasted

1 tbsp Dijon mustard

1 tbsp balsamic vinegar

3-4 tbsp olive oil

salt, to taste

Directions:

Prepare the dressing by combining mustard, lemon juice and olive oil.

Place walnuts on a baking tray and bake in a preheated to 400 F oven for 3-4 minutes, or until browned.

Mix radicchio, rocket, apples, onions and walnuts in a large salad bowl. Add the dressing; season with salt, toss to combine and serve.

Apple, Celery and Walnut Salad

Serves 4-5

Prep time 5 min

Ingredients

3 large apples, quartered, cores removed, thinly sliced

1 celery rib, thinly sliced

½ cup walnuts, chopped

1 red onion, thinly sliced

2 tbsp raisins

1/4 cup sunflower seeds

3 tbsp apple cider vinegar

2 tbsp olive oil

salt and black pepper, to taste

Directions:

Mix vinegar, olive oil, salt and pepper in a small bowl. Whisk until well combined.

Place apples, celery, onion, walnuts, raisins and sunflower seeds in a bigger salad bowl. Drizzle with dressing, toss and serve.

Fresh Greens Salad

Serves: 6-7

Prep time 5 min

Ingredients:

1 small red leaf lettuce, rinsed, dried and chopped

1 small green leaf lettuce, rinsed, dried and chopped

1/2 head endive, rinsed, dried and chopped

1 cup frisee lettuce leaves, rinsed, dried and chopped

3-4 fresh basil leaves, chopped

3-4 fresh mint leaves, chopped

2-3 green onions, chopped

1 tbsp chia seeds

4 tbsp olive oil

3-4 tbsp lemon juice

1 tbsp maple syrup

1 tsp mustard

salt, to taste

Directions:

Place the red and green leaf lettuce, frisee lettuce, endive, onions, basil and mint into a large salad bowl and toss lightly to combine.

Prepare the dressing by whisking lemon juice, mustard, olive oil and maple syrup. Pour it over the salad, toss to combine, sprinkle with chia seeds and season with salt to taste.

Beet and Lentil Salad

Serves 6

Prep time 5-6 min

Ingredients

1 can brown lentils, drained and rinsed

1 can pickled beets, drained and cut in cubes

5 oz baby rocket leaves

¼ cup walnuts, toasted and roughly chopped

4-5 green onions, chopped

1 garlic clove, crushed

3 tbsp olive oil

2 tbsp lemon juice

salt and black pepper, to taste

Directions:

Heat olive oil in a frying pan and gently sauté the green onions for 1-2 minutes or until softened. Add in garlic and lentils. Cook, for 2 minutes, then add in beets and cook for 2-3 minutes more.

Combine baby rocket, walnuts and lentil mixture in a large salad bowl. Sprinkle with lemon juice, toss gently to combine, and serve.

Beet and Bean Sprout Salad

Serves: 4-5

Prep time 5 min

Ingredients:

5-6 beet greens, cut in thin strips

2 tomatoes, sliced

1 cup bean sprouts, washed

3 tbsp roasted pumpkin seeds

1 tbsp grated lemon rind

2 garlic cloves, crushed

4 tbsp lemon juice

3 tbsp olive oil

1 tsp salt

Directions:

In a large bowl, toss together beet greens, bean sprouts, tomatoes and pumpkin seeds.

Mix oil and lemon juice with lemon rind, salt and garlic and pour over the salad. Serve chilled.

Roasted Vegetable Salad

Serves: 4

Prep time 25 min

Ingredients:

2 tomatoes, halved

1 medium zucchini, quartered

1 eggplant, ends trimmed, quartered

2 large red pepper, halved, deseeded, cut into strips

2-3 white mushrooms, halved

1 onion, quartered

1 tsp garlic powder

2 tbsp olive oil

for the dressing:

1 tbsp lemon juice

1 tbsp apple cider vinegar

2 tbsp olive oil

1 tsp sumac

5 tbsp crushed walnuts, to serve

Directions:

Whisk olive oil, lemon juice, vinegar and sumac in a bowl.

Preheat oven to 500 F. Place the zucchini, eggplant, peppers, onion, mushrooms and tomatoes on a lined baking sheet. Sprinkle with olive oil, season with salt, pepper and sumac and roast until golden, about 25 minutes.

Divide in 4-5 plates, top with crushed walnuts, drizzle with the dressing and serve.

Light Superfood Salad

Serves 4

Prep time 5 min

Ingredients

1 cup mixed green salad leaves

2 cups watercress, rinsed, patted dry and separated from roots

4-5 green onions, chopped

1 avocado, peeled and cubed

10 radishes, sliced

10 green olives, pitted and halved

for the dressing:

1 tbsp lemon juice

2 tbsp apple cider vinegar

2 tbsp olive oil

1 tbsp Dijon mustard

1/2 tsp dried mint

Directions:

Combine all salad ingredients in a large bowl.

In a medium bowl or cup, whisk lemon juice, vinegar, olive oil, mint and mustard until smooth. Pour over salad, toss, and serve.

Baby Spinach Salad

Serves: 4

Prep time 5 min

Ingredients:

1 bag baby spinach, washed and dried

1 red bell pepper, cut in slices

1 cup cherry tomatoes, cut in halves

1 small red onion, finely chopped

1 cup black olives, pitted

for the dressing:

1 tsp dried oregano

1 large garlic clove

3 tbsp red wine vinegar

4 tbsp olive oil

salt and black pepper, to taste

Directions:

Prepare the dressing by blending the garlic and oregano with olive oil and vinegar in a food processor.

Place the spinach leaves in a large salad bowl and toss with the dressing. Add the rest of the ingredients and give everything a toss again. Season to taste with black pepper and salt.

Green Bean and Radicchio Salad with Green Olive Dressing

Serves 4

Prep time 10 min

Ingredients

1 lb trimmed green beans, cut to 2-3 inch long pieces

1 radicchio, outer leaves removed, washed, dried

1 small red onion, finely cut

1 cup cherry tomatoes, halved

green olive dressing

1/2 cup green olives, pitted

1/3 cup olive oil

2 garlic cloves, chopped

black pepper and salt, to taste

Directions:

Roughly tear the radicchio leaves and place on a large serving platter.

Steam or boil green beans for about 3-4 minutes until crisp-tender. In a colander, wash with cold water to stop cooking, then pat dry and arrange over the radicchio leaves. Add in red onion and cherry tomatoes.

To make the green olive dressing, place the olives in a food processor and blend until finely chopped. Gradually add the oil and process until a smooth paste is formed. Taste and season with salt and pepper then spoon over salad and serve.

Cucumber Salad

Serves 4

Prep time 5 min

Ingredients:

2 medium cucumbers, sliced

a bunch of fresh dill

2 cloves garlic

3 tbsp white vinegar

5 tbsp olive oil

salt to taste

Directions:

Cut the cucumbers in rings and put arrange them on a plate. Add the finely cut dill, the pressed garlic and season with salt, vinegar and oil.

Mix well and serve cold.

Tomato Couscous Salad

Serves 2

Prep time 10 min

Ingredients:

1 cup medium couscous

1 cup hot water

2 ripe tomatoes, diced

1/2 red onion, finely cut

5 tbsp sunflower oil

4 tbsp lemon juice

1 tbsp dried mint

Directions:

Place the couscous in a large bowl. Boil water with one tablespoon of olive oil and pour over the couscous. Cover and set aside for 10 minutes.

Fluff couscous with a fork and when it is completely cold, stir in the tomatoes, onion and dry mint.

In a separate small bowl, combine the remaining olive oil, lemon juice and salt, add to the couscous, and stir until well combined.

Carrot Salad

Serves 4

Prep time 5 min

Ingredients:

4 carrots, shredded

1 apple, peeled, cored and shredded

2 garlic cloves, crushed

2 tbsp lemon juice

2 tbsp honey

salt and pepper to taste

Directions:

In a bowl, combine the shredded carrots, apple, lemon juice, honey, garlic, salt and pepper.

Toss and chill before serving.

Zucchini Pasta Salad

Serves 6

Prep time 20 min

Ingredients:

2 cups spiral pasta

2 zucchinis, sliced and halved

4 tomatoes, cut

1 cup white mushrooms, cut

1 small red onion, chopped

2 tbsp fresh basil leaves, chopped

3.5 oz blue cheese

2 tbsp sunflower oil

1 tbsp lemon juice

black pepper, to taste

Directions:

Cook pasta according to directions or until al dente. Drain, rinse with cold water and drain again.

Place zucchinis, tomatoes, mushrooms and onion in a large bowl. Add in pasta and mix gently.

Combine oil, lemon juice, basil, blue cheese and black pepper in a blender. Pour over salad. Toss gently and serve.

Granny's Salad

Serves 6

Prep time 20 min

Ingredients:

3 potatoes, boiled, diced

2 carrots, boiled, cut

1 cup canned green peas, drained

1 cup mayonnaise

5 pickled gherkins, chopped

black olives, to serve

salt to taste

Directions:

Boil the potatoes and carrots, then chop into small cubes. Put everything, except for the mayonnaise, in a serving bowl and mix.

Add salt to taste, then stir in the mayonnaise. Garnish with parsley and olives. Serve cold.

Buckwheat Salad with Asparagus and Roasted Peppers

Serves 4-5

Prep time 15 min

Ingredients:

1 cup buckwheat groats

1 3/4 cups vegetable broth

1/2 lb asparagus, trimmed and cut into 1 inch pieces

4 roasted red bell peppers, diced

2-3 spring onions, finely chopped

2 garlic cloves, crushed

1 tbsp red wine vinegar

3 tbsp olive oil

salt and black pepper, to taste

1/2 cup fresh parsley leaves, finely cut

Directions:

Heat a large dry saucepan and toast the buckwheat for about three minutes. Boil the vegetable broth and add it carefully to the buckwheat. Cover, reduce heat and simmer until the buckwheat is tender and all liquid is absorbed (5-7 minutes). Remove from heat, fluff with a fork and set aside to cool.

Rinse out the saucepan and then bring about an inch of water to a boil. Cook the asparagus in a steamer basket or colander, 2-3 minutes until tender. Transfer the asparagus in a large bowl along with the roasted peppers.

Add in the spring onions, garlic, red wine vinegar, salt, pepper and olive oil. Stir to combine. Add the buckwheat to the vegetable mixture.

Sprinkle with parsley and toss the salad gently. Serve at room temperature.

Roasted Broccoli Buckwheat Salad

Serves 4-5

Prep time 25 min

Ingredients:

1 cup buckwheat groats

1 3/4 cups water

1 head of broccoli, cut into small pieces

1 lb asparagus, trimmed and cut into 1 inch pieces

1/2 cup roasted cashews

1/2 cup basil leaves, minced

1/2 cup olive oil

2 garlic cloves, crushed

1 tsp salt

3 tbsp Parmesan cheese, grated, to serve

Directions:

Arrange vegetables on a baking sheet and drizzle with olive oil. Roast in a preheated to 350 F oven for about fifteen minutes or until tender.

Heat a large, dry saucepan and toast the buckwheat for about three minutes, or until it releases a nutty aroma. Boil the water and add it carefully to the buckwheat. Cover, reduce heat and simmer until buckwheat is tender and all liquid is absorbed (5-7 minutes).

Remove from heat, fluff with a fork and set aside to cool.

Prepare the dressing by blending basil leaves, olive oil, garlic, and salt.

Toss vegetables, buckwheat and dressing together in a salad bowl. Add in cashews and serve sprinkled with Parmesan cheese.

Soups

Fresh Asparagus Soup

Serves 4

Prep time 25 min

Ingredients

1 lb fresh asparagus, cut into pieces

1 small onion, chopped

3 garlic cloves, chopped

½ cup milk

4 cups vegetable broth

2 tbsp olive oil

lemon juice, to taste

Directions:

Sauté onion for 3-4 minutes, stirring. Add in garlic and sauté for a minute more. Add in asparagus and sauté for 3-4 minutes.

Add broth, season with salt and pepper and bring to a boil then reduce heat and simmer for 20 minutes. Set aside to cool, add milk, and blend, until smooth. Season with lemon juice and serve.

Broccoli and Potato Soup

Serves 4-5

Prep time 25 min

Ingredients:

1 lb broccoli, cut into florets

2 potatoes, peeled and chopped

1 onion, chopped

3 garlic cloves, crushed

4 cups water

2 tbsp olive oil

¼ tsp ground nutmeg

Directions:

Heat oil in a large saucepan over medium-high heat. Add in onion and garlic and sauté, stirring, for 3 minutes or until soft.

Add in broccoli, potato and 4 cups of cold water. Cover, bring to a boil, reduce heat and simmer, stirring, for 15 minutes, or until potatoes are tender.

Remove from heat and blend until smooth. Return to saucepan and cook until heated through. Season with nutmeg and black pepper and serve.

Moroccan Lentil Soup

Serves 6-7

Prep time 30 min

Ingredients:

1 cup red lentils

1 cup canned chickpeas, drained

1 onion, chopped

2 cloves garlic, minced

1 cup canned tomatoes, chopped

1 cup canned white beans, drained

3 carrots, diced

1 celery rib, diced

5 cups water

3 tbsp olive oil

1 tsp ginger, grated

1 tsp ground cardamom

1/2 tsp cumin

Directions:

In a large soup pot, sauté onions, garlic and ginger in olive oil for about 5 minutes. Add in water, lentils, chickpeas, white beans, tomatoes, carrots, celery, cardamom and cumin.

Bring to a boil for a few minutes then lower heat and simmer for half an hour or longer until the lentils are tender. Puree half the soup in a food processor or blender. Return the pureed soup to the pot, stir and serve.

Beetroot and Carrot Soup

Serves 5-6

Prep time 30 min

Ingredients:

4 beets, washed and peeled

2 carrots, peeled, chopped

2 potatoes, peeled, chopped

1 small onion, chopped

2 cups vegetable broth

2 cups water

3 tbsp olive oil

1 cup finely cut green onions, to serve

Directions:

Heat olive oil in a deep saucepan over medium-high heat and sauté the onion and carrot until tender. Add in beets, potatoes, broth and water.

Bring to the boil then reduce heat and simmer, partially covered, for 25 minutes, or until beets are tender.

Set aside to cool then blend in batches until smooth. Return soup to saucepan and cook, stirring, for 4-5 minutes, or until heated through. Season with salt and pepper and serve sprinkled with green onions.

Celery, Apple and Carrot Soup

Serves 4

Prep time 20 min

Ingredients:

2 celery ribs, chopped

1 large apple, chopped

1/2 small onion, chopped

3 carrots, chopped

2 garlic cloves, crushed

4 cups vegetable broth

3 tbsp olive oil

1 tsp ground ginger

salt and black pepper, to taste

Directions:

In a deep saucepan, heat olive oil over medium-high heat and sauté onion, garlic, celery and carrots for 3-4 minutes, stirring. Add in ginger, apple and vegetable broth.

Bring to a boil then reduce heat and simmer, covered, for 10 minutes. Blend until smooth and return to the pot.

Cook over medium-high heat until heated through. Season with salt and pepper to taste and serve.

Pumpkin and Bell Pepper Soup

Serves 4

Prep time 30 min

Ingredients:

1 medium leek, chopped

9 oz pumpkin, peeled, deseeded, cut into small cubes

1 red bell pepper, cut into small pieces

1 can tomatoes, undrained, crushed

3 cups vegetable broth

1/2 tsp cumin

salt and black pepper, to taste

Directions:

Heat the olive oil in a medium saucepan and sauté the leek for 4-5 minutes. Add in the pumpkin and bell pepper and cook, stirring, for 5 minutes. Add tomatoes, broth, and cumin and bring to a boil.

Cover, reduce heat to low, and simmer, stirring occasionally, for 25 minutes or until the vegetables are soft. Season with salt and pepper and leave aside to cool. Blend in batches and reheat to serve.

Spinach, Leek and Quinoa Soup

Serves 4-5

Prep time 30 min

Ingredients:

½ cup quinoa, very well washed

2 leeks halved lengthwise and sliced

1 onion, chopped

2 garlic cloves, chopped

1 can diced tomatoes, (15 oz), undrained

2 cups fresh spinach, cut

4 cups vegetable broth

2 tbsp olive oil

salt and pepper, to taste

Directions:

Heat olive oil in a large soup pot over medium heat and sauté onion for 2 minutes, stirring. Add in leeks and cook for another 2-3 minutes. Stir in garlic, salt and black pepper to taste. Add the vegetable broth, canned tomatoes and quinoa.

Bring to a boil then reduce heat and simmer for 15 minutes. Stir in spinach and cook for another 5 minutes.

Vegetable Quinoa Soup

Serves 6

Prep time 30 min

Ingredients:

½ cup quinoa

1/2 onion, chopped

1 potato, peeled and diced

1 carrot, diced

1 red bell pepper, chopped

2 tomatoes, chopped

1 small zucchini, peeled and diced

4 cups water

1 tsp dried oregano

3-4 tbsp olive oil

black pepper, to taste

2 tbsp fresh lemon juice

Directions:

Rinse quinoa very well in a fine mesh strainer under running water; set aside to drain.

Heat olive oil in a large soup pot and gently sauté the onion and carrot for 2-3 minutes, stirring every now and then. Add in potato, bell pepper, tomatoes, oregano and water.

Stir to combine, cover, and bring to a boil then lower heat and simmer for 10 minutes. Add in quinoa and zucchini; cover and simmer for 15 minutes or until the vegetables are tender. Add in lemon juice; stir to combine and serve.

Potato Soup

Serves 8

Prep time 30 min

Ingredients:

4-5 medium potatoes, cut into small cubes

2 carrots, chopped

1 zucchini, chopped

1 celery rib, chopped

3 cups water

3 tbsp olive oil

1 cup whole milk

1/2 tsp dried rosemary

salt to taste

black pepper to taste

a bunch of fresh parsley for garnish, finely cut

Directions:

Heat the olive oil over medium heat and sauté the vegetables for 2-3 minutes. Add 3 cups of water and rosemary and bring to a boil hen lower heat and simmer until all the vegetables are tender.

Blend soup in a blender until smooth. Add a cup of warm milk and blend some more. Serve warm, seasoned with black pepper and parsley sprinkled over each serving.

Spicy Carrot Soup

Serves 6-7

Prep time 30 min

Ingredients

10 carrots, peeled and chopped

2 medium onions, chopped

4-5 cups water

5 tbsp olive oil

2 cloves garlic, minced

1 red chili pepper, finely chopped

salt and pepper, to taste

1/2 cup heavy cream

1/2 bunch, fresh coriander, finely cut

Directions:

Heat olive oil in a large pot over medium heat and sauté the onions, carrots garlic and chili pepper for 2-3 minutes, stirring. Add in water and bring to a boil. Reduce heat to low and simmer for 25 minutes.

Transfer to a blender or food processor and blend until smooth. Return to the pot and continue cooking for a few more minutes. Stir in the cream and serve with coriander sprinkled over each serving.

Mushroom Soup

Serves 4

Prep time 30 min

Ingredients:

2 cups mushrooms, peeled and chopped

1 onion, chopped

2 cloves of garlic, crushed and chopped

1 tsp dried thyme

3 cups vegetable broth

salt and pepper to taste

3 tbsp sunflower or olive oil

Directions:

Sauté the onion and garlic in a large soup pot until transparent. Add in thyme and the mushrooms.

Sauté, stirring, for 5-6 minutes then add in vegetable broth and simmer for another 15 minutes. Blend, season and serve.

French Vegetable Soup

Serves 6

Prep time 30 min

Ingredients:

1 leek, thinly sliced

1 large zucchini, diced

1 cup green beans, cut

2 garlic cloves, cut

3 cups vegetable broth

1 can tomatoes, chopped

3.5 oz vermicelli, broken into small pieces

3 tbsp olive oil

salt and black pepper, to taste

4 tbsp freshly grated Parmesan cheese

Directions:

Heat olive oil in a large soup pot and sauté the leek, zucchini, green beans and garlic for about 3-4 minutes. Add in vegetable broth and stir in the tomatoes.

Bring to a boil, reduce heat and season with black pepper and salt to taste. Simmer for 15 minutes or until the vegetables are tender, but still holding their shape.

Stir in the vermicelli. Cover again and simmer for 5 more minutes. Serve warm sprinkled with Parmesan cheese.

Minted Pea Soup

Serves 4

Prep time 30 min

Ingredients:

1 onion, finely chopped

2 garlic cloves, finely chopped

3 cups vegetable broth

1/3 cup mint leaves

2 lb green peas, frozen

3 tbsp sunflower oil

1/4 cup yogurt, to serve

small mint leaves, to serve

Directions:

Heat oil in a large saucepan over medium-high heat and sauté onion and garlic for 5 minutes or until soft.

Add vegetable broth and bring to a boil then add mint and peas. Cover, reduce heat and cook for 20 minutes or until peas are tender but still green. Remove from heat.

Set aside to cool slightly then blend soup, in batches, until smooth. Return soup to saucepan over medium-low heat and cook until heated through.

Season with salt and pepper. Serve topped with yogurt, pepper and mint leaves.

Italian Minestrone

Serves 6-7

Prep time 30 min

Ingredients:

1/4 cabbage, chopped

2 carrots, chopped

1 celery rib, thinly sliced

1 small onion, chopped

2 garlic cloves, chopped

2 tbsp olive oil

2 cups water

1 can tomatoes, diced, undrained

1 cup fresh spinach, torn

1/2 cup pasta, cooked

black pepper and salt to taste

Directions:

In a soup pot, sauté carrots, cabbage, celery, onion and garlic in oil for 5 minutes. Add in water, tomatoes and bring to a boil.

Reduce heat and simmer uncovered, for 20 minutes or until the vegetables are tender.

Stir in spinach, pasta and season with pepper and salt to taste.

Garlicky Cauliflower Soup

Serves 8

Prep time 30 min

Ingredients:

1 large onion finely cut

1 medium head cauliflower, chopped

2-3 garlic cloves, minced

2 cups water

1/2 cup whole cream

4 tbsp olive oil

salt, to taste

black pepper, to taste

Directions:

Heat the olive oil in a large pot over medium heat, and sauté the onion, cauliflower and garlic.

Stir in the water, and bring to a boil. Reduce heat, cover, and simmer for 25 minutes.

Remove from heat, add cream, and blend in a blender. Season with salt and pepper and serve.

Spinach Soup

Serves 6

Prep time 30 min

Ingredients:

1 lb spinach, frozen

1/4 cup white rice

1 large onion or 4-5 spring onions, finely cut

1 carrot, chopped

4 cups water

3-4 tbsp olive oil

1-2 cloves garlic, crushed

1 tsp paprika

black pepper, to taste

salt, to taste

Directions:

Heat the oil in a cooking pot, add the onion and carrot and sauté together for a few minutes, until just softened. Add in garlic, paprika and rice and stir.

Add the spinach and about 4 cups of hot water and season with salt and pepper.

Bring to a boil, reduce the heat and simmer for around 20 minutes.

Gazpacho

Serves 6-7

Prep time 5 min

Ingredients:

2.25 lb tomatoes, peeled and halved

1 onion, sliced

1 green pepper, sliced

1 large cucumber, peeled and sliced

2 cloves garlic

4 tbsp olive oil

1 tbsp apple cider vinegar

salt, to taste

to garnish

1/2 onion, chopped

1 green pepper, chopped

1 cucumber, chopped

Directions:

Place the tomatoes, garlic, onion, green pepper, cucumber, salt, olive oil and vinegar in a blender or food processor and puree until smooth, adding small amounts of cold water if needed to achieve desired consistency.

Serve the soup chilled, topped with the chopped onion, green pepper and cucumber.

Cold Cucumber Soup

Serves 6

Prep time 5 min

Ingredients:

1 large or two small cucumbers

2 cups yogurt

4-5 cloves garlic, crushed or chopped

1 cup cold water

4 tbsp sunflower or olive oil

1 cup fresh dill, finely chopped

1/2 cup crushed walnuts

Directions:

Wash the cucumber, peel and cut it into small cubes.

In a large bowl, dilute the yogurt with water to taste, add the cucumber and garlic, stirring well.

Add salt to taste, garnish with the dill and the crushed walnuts, and put in the fridge to cool.

Main Dishes

Delicious Skinny Pizza

Serves: 4

Prep time 30 min

Ingredients:

1 store-bought or homemade dough

1/3 cup onion, finely chopped

1 cup mushrooms, chopped

1/2 cup red bell pepper, chopped

1/2 cup tomato sauce

4-5 green or black olives

2 tbsp olive oil

1/2 tsp oregano

1 tsp dried basil

1/2 tsp garlic powder

salt and black pepper, to taste

a handful of baby rocket leaves, to serve

Directions:

Heat a large skillet on medium heat and sauté the onion and pepper for 1-2 minutes. Add in the mushrooms, garlic powder, oregano and basil and sauté for 2 minutes more. Season with salt and black pepper to taste.

Roll out dough onto a floured surface and transfer to a parchment-lined 12 inch round baking sheet or pizza stone.

Top with fresh or canned tomato sauce, the sautéed vegetables and the olives.

Bake for 30 minutes in a preheated to 450 F oven or until the crust is golden brown and the sauce is bubbly. Let rest for 5 minutes before cutting, top with rocket leaves, and serve.

Quick Quinoa Chilli

Serves: 4-5

Prep time 30 min

Ingredients:

1 cup quinoa, rinsed

2 cups vegetable broth

1 small onion, finely cut

2 cloves garlic, chopped

1 yellow pepper, chopped

1 large tomato, diced

1 can black beans, well rinsed and drained

1 tbsp tomato paste

1 tbsp paprika

1 tsp chilli powder

1/2 tsp ground cumin

2 tbsp olive oil

¼ cup chopped fresh coriander, to serve

Directions:

In a deep casserole dish, heat the olive oil over medium heat. Add in the onion, pepper, tomato and garlic and sauté, stirring, for 2-3 minutes.

Add in the chilli powder, cumin and paprika and sauté for another minute. Add in vegetable broth, tomato paste, beans and quinoa and stir to combine.

Bring the chili to a boil then reduce heat and simmer, covered, for about 15 minutes. Serve sprinkled with fresh coriander.

Avocado and Rocket Pasta

Serves: 4

Prep time 30 min

Ingredients:

3 cups cooked small pasta

½ cup canned sweet corn

1 large avocado, peeled and diced

1 cup baby rocket leaves

5-6 fresh basil leaves, chopped

3 tbsp olive oil

3 tbsp lemon juice

Directions:

Whisk olive oil, lemon juice and basil in a small bowl. Season with salt and pepper to taste.

Combine pasta, avocado, corn and baby rocket. Add oil mixture and toss to combine.

Delicious Broccoli Pasta

Serves: 4

Prep time 30 min

Ingredients:

1 cup small pasta

2 cups broccoli florets

1/3 cup walnuts, chopped

2 garlic cloves, chopped

10 cherry tomatoes, halved

5-6 fresh basil leaves

3 tbsp olive oil

3 tbsp lemon juice

Directions:

Combine olive oil, lemon juice, garlic, walnuts, basil and broccoli in blender. Season with salt and pepper to taste and blend until smooth.

In a large pot of boiling salted water, cook pasta according to package instructions. Drain and set aside in a large bowl.

Combine pasta, broccoli mixture and cherry tomatoes, toss, and serve.

Creamy Butternut Squash Spaghetti

Serves 4

Prep time 30 min

Ingredients

12 oz spaghetti

3 cups butternut squash, peeled, cut into small pieces

1/2 small onion, chopped

2 garlic cloves, chopped

1 carrot, cut

1 cup vegetable broth

5-6 fresh sage, chopped

1 tsp paprika

3 tbsp olive oil

salt and black pepper, to taste

Directions:

Heat olive oil in a large skillet and cook the onions, garlic and carrot until soft. Add in paprika and the pumpkin and mix well. Stir in vegetable broth and bring the mixture to a boil, then reduce heat and simmer until pumpkin is soft, about 15 to 20 minutes. Set aside to cool.

In a large pot of boiling salted water, cook spaghetti according to package instructions. Drain and set aside in a large bowl.

Once the pumpkin mixture has cooled, purée it until smooth, then season with salt and pepper to taste.

Combine spaghetti, pumpkin mixture and fresh sage leaves, toss, and serve.

Zucchini Bake

Serves 4

Prep time 30 min

Ingredients:

5 medium zucchinis, grated

1 carrot, grated

1 small tomato, diced

1 onion, halved, thinly sliced

2 garlic cloves, crushed

1 cup self-raising flour, sifted

5 eggs, lightly whisked

1/2 cup fresh dill, finely cut

1 cup grated feta cheese

1/2 cup sunflower oil

2 cups yogurt, to serve

Directions:

Preheat oven to 350 F. Grease and line a round, 8 inch base, baking dish.

Combine zucchinis, carrot, tomato, onion, garlic and dill in a bowl. Add flour, eggs, oil and cheese. Season and stir until well combined.

Bake for 30 minutes. Serve with yogurt.

Spinach with Eggs

Serves 2

Prep time 20 min

Ingredients:

1 lb spinach, fresh or frozen

1 onion, finely cut

4 eggs

3 tbsp olive oil

1/4 tsp cumin

1 tsp paprika

salt and pepper, to taste

1 cup yogurt, to serve

Directions:

In a skillet, heat olive oil on medium-low. Gently sauté the onion for 2-3 minutes. Add in paprika and cumin and stir to combine.

Add spinach and sauté until it wilts. Season with salt and black pepper to taste.

Make 4 holes in the spinach for the eggs. Break an egg into each hole. Cover and cook until eggs are cooked through. Serve with a dollop of yogurt.

Artichoke and Onion Frittata

Serves 4

Prep time 15 min

Ingredients

1 small onion, chopped

1 cup marinated artichoke hearts, drained

6 eggs

1 garlic clove, crushed

1 tbsp olive oil

salt and black pepper, to taste

1 cup fresh parsley, finely cut, to serve

Directions:

Heat oil in a non-stick oven pan over medium heat and sauté the onion stirring occasionally, for 5-6 minutes or until golden brown. Add artichokes and cook for 2 minutes or until heated through.

Whisk eggs with garlic until combined well. Season with salt and pepper. Pour the egg mixture over the artichoke mixture. Reduce heat, cover and cook for 10 minutes or until frittata is set around the edge but still runny in the center.

Place pan into preheated oven and cook 4-5 until golden brown. Remove from oven and cut into wedges. Serve sprinkled with parsley.

Tomato and Leek Stew

Serves 5-6

Prep time 30 min

Ingredients:

1 lb leeks, cut into rings

1/2 cup vegetable broth

2 tbsp tomato paste

4 tbsp sunflower oil

1 tbsp dried mint

salt to taste

fresh ground pepper to taste

Directions:

Heat oil in a heavy wide saucepan or sauté pan. Add in leeks, salt, pepper, and sauté, stirring, for 5 minutes. Add in vegetable broth and bring to a boil.

Cover, and simmer over low heat, stirring often, for about 10-15 minutes or until leeks are tender. Gently stir in tomato paste and dried mint, raise heat to medium, uncover and simmer for 5 minutes.

Okra and Tomato Casserole

Serves 4-5

Prep time 30 min

Ingredients:

1 lb okra, stem ends trimmed

4 large tomatoes, cut into wedges

3 garlic cloves, chopped

3 tbsp olive oil

1 tsp salt

black pepper, to taste

Directions:

In a large casserole, mix together trimmed okra, sliced tomatoes, olive oil and chopped garlic. Add salt and pepper and toss to combine.

Bake in a preheated to 350 F oven for 45 minutes, or until the okra is tender.

Creamy Green Pea and Rice Casserole

Serves 4

Prep time 30 min

Ingredients

1 onion, very finely cut

1 bag frozen peas

2-3 garlic cloves, chopped

3-4 mushrooms, chopped

1/2 cup white rice

1 cup water

4 tbsp olive oil

1/2 cup sour cream

2/3 cup grated Parmesan cheese

1/2 cup fresh dill, finely cut

salt and black pepper, to taste

Directions:

In a deep ovenproof casserole dish, heat olive oil and sauté the onions, garlic and mushrooms for 2-3 minutes. Add in rice and cook, stirring, for 1 minute. Add in a cup of warm water, the frozen peas, and the dill.

Stir to combine, and bake in a preheated to 350 F oven, for 20 minutes.

Stir in sour cream, sprinkle with Parmesan cheese, bake for 2-3 more minutes and serve.

Zucchini and Almond Pasta

Serves 4

Prep time 30 min

Ingredients:

2 cups fusilli (or other short pasta)

1 tbsp olive oil

2 garlic cloves, crushed

2 zucchinis, coarsely grated

1/2 cup slivered almonds, lightly toasted

2 tbs chopped fresh parsley

1 tbs chopped mint leaves

1/2 cup sour cream

2 tbs grated Parmesan cheese

Directions:

Cook the pasta according to package instructions until al dente.

Meanwhile, heat oil in a large frying pan over medium heat and sauté the garlic and for 30 seconds. Add the zucchinis and sauté, stirring occasionally, for 5 minutes or until all the liquid has evaporated. Add almonds and herbs, stir to combine and season with salt and pepper.

Drain the cooked pasta, add to the pan together with the sour cream and Parmesan cheese and toss to combine.

Poached Eggs with Feta and Yogurt

Serves 4

Prep time 15 min

Ingredients:

12 eggs

2 cups plain yogurt

10 oz feta cheese, crumbled

2 tsp paprika

3 cloves garlic

2 oz butter

Directions:

Crush the garlic and stir together with the yogurt and the grated cheese. Divide the mixture into four plates.

Poach the eggs, take them out with a serving spoon and place three eggs on top of the mixture in each plate.

Brown the butter together with paprika and pour one quarter over each plate before serving.

Beet Fries

Serves: 4

Prep time 30 min

Ingredients:

3 beets, cut in strips

3 tbsp olive oil

1 cup finely cut spring onions

2 garlic cloves, crushed

1 tsp salt

Directions:

Line a baking dish with baking paper. Wash and peel the beets then cut them in strips similar to French fries. Toss the beets with olive oil, spring onions, garlic and salt.

Arrange beets on a prepared baking sheet and place in a preheated to 425 F oven for 25-30 minutes, flipping halfway through.

Grilled Vegetable Skewers

Serves: 4

Prep time 30 min

Ingredients:

1 red pepper

1 green pepper

3 zucchinis, halved lengthwise and sliced

3 onions, quartered

12 medium mushrooms, whole

2 garlic cloves, crushed

2 tbsp olive oil

1 tsp summer savory

1 tsp cumin

1 spring fresh rosemary, leaves only

salt and ground black pepper, to taste

Directions:

Deseed and cut the peppers into chunks. Divide between 6 skewers threading alternately with the zucchinis, onions and mushrooms. Set aside the skewers in a shallow plate.

Mix the crushed garlic with the herbs, cumin, salt, black pepper and olive oil. Roll each skewer in the mixture.

Bake the vegetable skewers on a hot barbecue or char grill, turning occasionally, until slightly charred.

Mish-Mash

Serves 5-6

Prep time 15 min

Ingredients:

1 small onion, finely cut

1 green bell pepper, chopped

2 red bell peppers, chopped

4 tomatoes, cubed

2 garlic cloves, crushed

8 eggs

9 oz feta cheese, crumbled

4 tbsp olive oil

1/2 cup parsley, finely cut

black pepper

salt

Directions:

In a large pan, sauté onion over medium heat until transparent. Reduce heat and add in bell peppers and garlic. Continue cooking until soft.

Add the tomatoes and continue simmering until the mixture is almost dry. Add the cheese and all eggs and cook until well mixed and not too liquid.

Season with black pepper and remove from heat. Sprinkle with parsley.

Eggs and Feta Cheese Stuffed Peppers

Serves 4

Prep time 30 min

Ingredients:

8 red bell peppers

6 eggs

4 oz feta cheese

2 cups breadcrumbs

sunflower oil, for frying

a bunch of parsley, finely cut, to serve

Directions:

Grill the peppers or roast them in the oven at 480 F. Peel and deseed the peppers. Mix the crumbled feta cheese with 4 beaten eggs.

Stuff the peppers with the cheese mixture.

Whisk the remaining two eggs. Roll each stuffed pepper first in breadcrumbs then dip in the beaten eggs.

Fry in hot oil turning once. Serve sprinkled with parsley.

Feta Cheese Baked in Foil

Serves 4

Prep time 15 min

Ingredients:

1 lb hard feta cheese

3 oz butter

1 tbsp paprika

1 tsp summer savory

Directions:

Cut the cheese into four medium-thick slices and place on sheets of butter-lined foil or parchment paper.

Place a bit of butter on top of each feta cheese piece, sprinkle with paprika and summer savory and wrap the foil.

Place in a tray and bake for 10 minutes in a moderate oven. Serve wrapped in the foil.

Breaded Cheese

Serves 4

Prep time 20 min

Ingredients:

1 lb feta cheese, cut in 4 slices

2 eggs, beaten

2 tbsp flour

3-4 tbsp breadcrumbs

vegetable oil for frying

Directions:

Cut the cheese in four equal slices. Dip each slice first in cold water, then roll in the flour, then in the beaten eggs, and finally in the breadcrumbs.

Fry in preheated oil for 1-2 minutes each side. Serve warm.

Spinach with Rice

Serves 4-5

Prep time 30 min

Ingredients:

3-4 cups fresh spinach, washed, drained and chopped

1/2 cup rice

1 onion, chopped

1 carrot, chopped

1/4 cup olive oil

2 cups water

salt and pepper, to taste

yogurt, to serve

Directions:

Heat the oil in a large skillet and saute the onions and the carrot for 1-2 minutes, stirring.

Add in paprika and the washed and drained rice and stir to combine. Add two cups of warm water, stirring constantly as the rice absorbs it, and simmer for 15 more minutes.

Wash the spinach well and cut it in strips then add to the rice. Cook for 5 more minutes or until it wilts. Remove from the heat and season to taste. Serve with yogurt.

Breakfasts and Desserts

Berry Quinoa Breakfast

Serves 2

Prep time 30 min

Ingredients:

½ cup quinoa

1 cup milk

¼ cup fresh blueberries or raspberries

1 tbsp walnuts or almonds, chopped

Directions:

Wash quinoa and cook according to package directions. Combine it with milk in and bring to a boil.

Cover, reduce heat and simmer for 15 minutes. When ready add walnuts and cinnamon, place a portion of the quinoa into a bowl and top with fresh blueberries.

Citrus Quinoa Breakfast

Serves: 2

Prep time 15 min

Ingredients:

½ cup quinoa

1 cup water

1 orange, peeled, cut into bite-sized pieces

2 tbsp blanched almonds, chopped

2 tbsp cranberries

1 tsp lemon zest

½ tsp vanilla

Directions:

Rinse quinoa and drain. Place water and quinoa into a small saucepan and bring to a boil. Add vanilla and lemon zest.

Reduce heat to low and simmer for about 15 minutes stirring often. When ready, place a portion of the quinoa into a bowl and top with orange segments, cranberries and almonds.

Avocado and Olive Paste on Toasted Rye Bread

Serves: 4

Prep time 5 min

Ingredients:

1 avocado, peeled and finely chopped

2 tbsp black olive paste

1 tbsp lemon juice

Directions:

Mash avocados with a fork or potato masher until almost smooth. Add the black olive paste and lemon juice. Season with salt and pepper to taste. Stir to combine.

Toast 4 slices of rye bread until golden. Spoon 1/4 of the avocado mixture onto each slice of bread.

Avocado, Feta and Tomato Sandwiches

Serves: 2

Prep time 5 min

Ingredients:

4 slices wholewheat bread

1 tbsp basil pesto

2 slices feta cheese

2 large leaves lettuce

1/2 tomato, thinly sliced

1/2 avocado, peeled and sliced

Directions:

Spread pesto on the four slices of bread.

Layer two slices with one lettuce leaf, two slices tomato, two slices avocado and two slices feta cheese.

Top with remaining bread slices. Cut sandwiches in half and serve.

Avocado and Chickpea Sandwiches

Serves 4

Prep time 5 min

Ingredients:

4 slices rye bread

1/2 can chickpeas, drained

1 avocado

2-3 green onions, finely chopped

1/2 tomato, thinly sliced

1/3 tsp cumin

salt, to taste

Directions:

Mash the avocado and chickpeas with a fork or potato masher until smooth. Add in green onions, cumin and salt and combine well.

Spread this mixture on the four slices of bread. Top each slice with tomato and serve.

French Toast

Serves 4

Prep time 30 min

Ingredients:

8 slices stale bread

4 eggs, beaten

2/3 cup milk

1/2 cup sunflower oil

Directions:

Slice the bread into thin 1/2 inch slices. Dip first in milk, then in the beaten eggs.

Fry in hot oil. Serve hot, sprinkled with sugar, honey, jam, feta cheese or whatever topping you prefer.

Quick Peach Tarts

Serves 4

Prep time 15 min

Ingredients:

1 sheet frozen ready-rolled puff pastry

1/4 cup light cream cheese spread

1 1/2 tablespoons raw sugar

pinch of cinnamon

4 peaches, peeled, halved, stones removed, sliced

Directions:

Preheat oven to 350 F. Line a baking tray with non-stick baking paper. Cut pastry into 4 squares. Place onto prepared tray.

Using a spoon, mix cream cheese, one tablespoon of sugar, vanilla and cinnamon. Spread over pastry squares. Arrange peach slices over top.

Bake for 10 minutes or until golden. Sprinkle with remaining sugar and serve.

FREE BONUS RECIPES: 10 Ridiculously Easy Jam and Jelly Recipes Anyone Can Make

A Different Strawberry Jam

Makes 6-7 11 oz jars

Ingredients:

4 lb fresh small strawberries (stemmed and cleaned)

5 cups sugar

1 cup water

2 tbsp lemon juice or 1 tsp citric acid

Directions:

Mix water and sugar and bring to the boil. Simmer sugar syrup for 5-6 minutes then slowly drop in the cleaned strawberries. Stir and bring to the boil again. Lower heat and simmer, stirring and skimming any foam off the top once or twice.

Drop a small amount of the jam on a plate and wait a minute to see if it has thickened. If it has gelled enough, turn off the heat. If not, keep boiling and test every 5 minutes until ready. Two or three minutes before you remove the jam from the heat, add lemon juice or citric acid and stir well.

Ladle the hot jam in the jars until 1/8-inch from the top. Place the lid on top and flip the jar upside down. Continue until all of the jars are filled and upside down. Allow the jam to cool completely before turning right-side up. Press on the lid to check and see if it has sealed. If one of the jars lids doesn't pop up- the jar is not sealed–store it in a refrigerator.

Raspberry Jam

Makes 4-5 11 oz jars

Ingredients:

4 cups raspberries

4 cups sugar

1 tsp vanilla extract

1/2 tsp citric acid

Directions:

Gently wash and drain the raspberries. Lightly crush them with a potato masher, food mill or a food processor. Do not puree, it is better to have bits of fruit. Sieve half of the raspberry pulp to remove some of the seeds.

Combine sugar and raspberries in a wide, thick-bottomed pot and bring mixture to a full rolling boil, stirring constantly. Skim any scum or foam that rises to the surface. Boil until the jam sets.

Test by putting a small drop on a cold plate – if the jam is set, it will wrinkle when given a small poke with your finger. Add citric acid, vanilla, and stir. Simmer for 2-3 minutes more, then ladle into hot jars. Flip upside down or process 10 minutes in boiling water.

Raspberry-Peach Jam

Makes 4-5 11 oz jars

Ingredients:

2 lb peaches

1 1/2 cup raspberries

4 cups sugar

1 tsp citric acid

Directions:

Wash and slice the peaches. Clean the raspberries and combine them with the peaches is a wide, heavy-bottomed saucepan. Cover with sugar and set aside for a few hours or overnight.

Bring the fruit and sugar to a boil over medium heat, stirring occasionally. Remove any foam that rises to the surface.

Boil until the jam sets. Add citric acid and stir. Simmer for 2-3 minutes more, then ladle into hot jars. Flip upside down or process 10 minutes in boiling water.

Blueberry Jam

Makes 4-5 11 oz jars

Ingredients:

4 cups granulated sugar

3 cups blueberries (frozen and thawed or fresh)

3/4 cup honey

2 tbsp lemon juice

1 tsp lemon zest

Directions:

Gently wash and drain the blueberries. Lightly crush them with a potato masher, food mill or a food processor. Add the honey, lemon juice, and lemon zest, then bring to a boil over medium-high heat.

Boil for 10-15 minutes, stirring from time to time. Boil until the jam sets.

Test by putting a small drop on a cold plate – if the jam is set, it will wrinkle when given a small poke with your finger. Skim off any foam, then ladle the jam into jars. Seal, flip upside down or process for 10 minutes in boiling water.

Triple Berry Jam

Makes 4-5 11 oz jars

Ingredients:

1 cup strawberries

1 cup raspberries

2 cups blueberries

4 cups sugar

1 tsp citric acid

Directions:

Mix berries and add sugar. Set aside for a few hours or overnight.

Bring the fruit and sugar to the boil over medium heat, stirring frequently. Remove any foam that rises to the surface. Boil until the jam sets. Add citric acid, salt and stir.

Simmer for 2-3 minutes more, then ladle into hot jars. Flip upside down or process 10 minutes in boiling water.

Red Currant Jelly

Makes 6-7 11 oz jars

Ingredients:

2 lb fresh red currants

1/2 cup water

3 cups sugar

1 tsp citric acid

Directions:

Place the currants into a large pot, and crush with a potato masher or berry crusher. Add in water, and bring to a boil. Simmer for 10 minutes.

Strain the fruit through a jelly or cheese cloth and measure out 4 cups of the juice. Pour the juice into a large saucepan, and stir in the sugar. Bring to full rolling boil, then simmer for 20-30 minutes, removing any foam that may rise to the surface. When the jelly sets, ladle in hot jars, flip upside down or process in boiling water for 10 minutes.

White Cherry Jam

Makes 3-4 11 oz jars

Ingredients:

2 lb cherries

3 cups sugar

2 cups water

1 tsp citric acid

Directions:

Wash and stone cherries. Combine water and sugar and bring to the boil.

Boil for 5-6 minutes then remove from heat and add cherries. Bring to a rolling boil and cook until set. Add citric acid, stir and boil 1-2 minutes more.

Ladle in hot jars, flip upside down or process in boiling water for 10 minutes.

Cherry Jam

Makes 3-4 11 oz jars

Ingredients:

2 lb fresh cherries, pitted, halved

4 cups sugar

1/2 cup lemon juice

Directions:

Place the cherries in a large saucepan. Add sugar and set aside for an hour. Add the lemon juice and place over low heat. Cook, stirring occasionally, for 10 minutes or until sugar dissolves.

Increase heat to high and bring to a rolling boil.

Cook for 5-6 minutes or until jam is set. Remove from heat and ladle hot jam into jars, seal and flip upside down.

Oven Baked Ripe Figs Jam

Makes 3-4 11 oz jars

Ingredients:

2 lb ripe figs

2 cups sugar

1 ½ cups water

2 tbsp lemon juice

Directions:

Arrange the figs in a Dutch oven, if they are very big, cut them in halves. Add sugar and water and stir well. Bake at 350 F for about one and a half hours. Do not stir.

You can check the readiness by dropping a drop of the syrup in a cup of cold water – if it falls to the bottom without dissolving, the jam is ready. If the drop dissolves before falling, you can bake it a little longer.

Take out of the oven, add lemon juice and ladle in the warm jars. Place the lids on top and flip the jars upside down. Allow the jam to cool completely before turning right-side up.

If you want to process the jams - place them into a large pot, cover the jars with water by at least 2 inches and bring to a boil. Boil for 10 minutes, remove the jars and sit to cool.

Quince Jam

Makes 5-6 11 oz jars

Ingredients:

4 lb quinces

5 cups sugar

2 cups water

1 tsp lemon zest

3 tbsp lemon juice

Directions:

Combine water and sugar in a deep, thick-bottomed saucepan and bring it to the boil. Simmer, stirring until the sugar has completely dissolved.

Rinse the quinces, cut in half, and discard the cores. Grate the quinces, using a cheese grater or a blender to make it faster. Quince flesh tends to darken very quickly, so it is good to do this as fast as possible. Add the grated quinces to the sugar syrup and cook uncovered, stirring occasionally until the jam turns pink and thickens to desired consistency, about 40 minutes. Drop a small amount of the jam on a plate and wait a minute to see if it has thickened.

If it has gelled enough, turn off the heat. If not, keep boiling and test every 2-3 minutes until ready. Two or three minutes before you remove the jam from the heat, add lemon juice and lemon zest and stir well.

Ladle in hot, sterilized jars and flip upside down.

About the Author

Vesela lives in Bulgaria with her family of six (including the Jack Russell Terrier). Her passion is going green in everyday life and she loves to prepare homemade cosmetic and beauty products for all her family and friends.

Vesela has been publishing her cookbooks for over a year now. If you want to see other healthy family recipes that she has published, together with some natural beauty books, you can check out her Author Page on Amazon.

34152545R00058

Printed in Great Britain
by Amazon